Recipe

Hacks

for

Sriracha

Hot Chili Sauce

Laura Sommers is **The Recipe Lady!**

She is the #1 Best Selling Author of over 80 recipe books.

She is a loving wife and mother who lives on a small farm in Baltimore County, Maryland and has a passion for all things domestic especially when it comes to saving money. She has a profitable eBay business and is a couponing addict. Follow her tips and tricks to learn how to make delicious meals on a budget, save money or to learn the latest life hack!

Visit her Amazon Author Page to see her latest books:

amazon.com/author/laurasommers

Visit the Recipe Lady's blog for even more great recipes and to learn which books are **FREE** for download each week:

http://the-recipe-lady.blogspot.com/

Subscribe to The Recipe Lady blog through Amazon and have recipes and updates sent directly to your Kindle:

The Recipe Lady Blog through Amazon

Laura Sommers is also an Extreme Couponer and Penny Hauler! If you would like to find out how to get things for **FREE** with coupons or how to get things for only a **PENNY**, then visit her couponing blog **Penny Items and Freebies**

http://penny-items-and-freebies.blogspot.com/

Introduction

Sriracha is a type of hot sauce or chili sauce made from a paste of chili peppers, distilled vinegar, garlic, sugar, and salt. This red hot sauce was invented by Huy Fong Foods and it comes in a bottle with a distinctive white rooster on the front. For this reason, many people refer to it as "Rooster Sauce."

Its popularity among hot sauce enthusiasts has led to many recipes being created with Sriracha as the defining ingredient. But if you love Sriracha and do not know how to use it beyond some basic recipes, then fear not. Here is a cookbook full of mouth watering meals and dishes to make using Sriracha hot chili sauce. Your meals will never be boring if you know how to Hack It!

Avocado Toast with Eggs and Sriracha

Ingredients:

2 slices italian or french bread, toasted
1 ripe avocado
2 eggs
coarse salt and pepper
Sriracha

Directions:

1. Place a non-stick frying pan over medium-low heat.
2. Crack the eggs into the pan, season with salt and pepper and cover. Cook until the whites are cooked through and yolk is still runny.
3. Meanwhile, mash half of the avocado with a fork. Season with salt. Spread half of the avocado mash onto each slice of toast. Then, place the eggs on top of each slice of toast.
4. Drizzle each egg with Sriracha to taste. Serve.

Sriracha Aioli

Goes great with crabcakes

Ingredients:

1 cup mayonnaise
2 tbsps. sriracha hot sauce
1 lime, juiced

Directions:

1. Stir mayonnaise and sriracha hot sauce together in a bowl until the color is consistent; add lime juice and stir.

Sriracha Biscuits

Ingredients:

2 1/4 cups self-rising flour
1 cup half-and-half
1/2 cup vegetable oil
1 tbsp. Sriracha hot sauce
1 tbsp. melted butter
Salt to taste

Directions:

1. Preheat oven to 425 degrees F (220 degrees C).
2. Stir flour, half-and-half, vegetable oil, and Sriracha sauce together in a bowl to form a lumpy dough.
3. Roll dough into 2-inch balls and place on a baking sheet.
4. Bake biscuits in the preheated oven until golden brown, about 15 minutes.
5. Brush melted butter and sprinkle salt on top of each biscuit.

Sriracha Pickled Eggs

Ingredients:

1 1/2 cups white vinegar
1 cup water
1 small onion, sliced
1/3 cup sriracha hot sauce
1 tsp. sea salt
12 hard-boiled eggs, peeled

Directions:

1. Combine vinegar, water, onion, sriracha hot sauce, and sea salt in a saucepan; bring to a simmer.
2. Remove saucepan from heat and cool liquid slightly.
3. Place eggs in a 1-quart jar.
4. Pour vinegar mixture over eggs.
5. Seal jar and refrigerate, occasionally shaking jar, for at least 2 days.

Sriracha Cheese Bread

Ingredients:

1/4 cup warm water (100 to 110 degrees F/40 to 45 degrees C)
1 (.25 oz.) package active dry yeast
1 tsp. honey
1/2 cup milk
1/4 cup Sriracha sauce
1/4 cup warm water (100 - 110 degrees F/40 - 45 degrees C)
1 egg, lightly beaten
1 cup white whole wheat flour
1/2 tsp. salt
1/2 cup shredded sharp Cheddar cheese
2 1/2 cups bread flour
1 tbsp. butter

Directions:

1. Combine 1/4 cup warm water, yeast, and honey in work bowl of a stand mixer, stirring to dissolve honey.
2. Let stand until yeast forms a creamy layer, about 10 minutes. Beat milk, chile-garlic sauce, and 1/4 cup warm water into yeast mixture; mix in egg.
3. Beat white whole wheat flour into liquid ingredients on low speed until flour is moistened; let stand 10 minutes for flour to absorb moisture. Add salt, Cheddar cheese, and 2 cups bread flour to bowl and mix until thoroughly incorporated.
4. Continue to beat remaining bread flour into dough, 1 tbsp. at a time, until the dough forms a ball and separates from the side of the mixing bowl. Add
5. Set the mixer to medium-low speed and knead for 10 minutes.
6. Dough should be slightly sticky.
7. Shape dough into a ball and place into an oiled bowl; turn dough ball around in the bowl to coat dough lightly with oil.
8. Cover with a cloth and set into a warm place to rise until doubled, 1 hour to 1 hour and 15 minutes.
9. Gently punch down dough to break bubbles and pat out on a floured work surface to a 9x12-inch rectangle.
10. Roll dough tightly in a spiral, starting at a 9-inch edge; pinch seams together to form a log. Place dough into a 5x9-inch loaf pan with seam side down and tuck ends of dough underneath neatly.

11. Cover with a cloth and let rise until dough top clears the sides of the pan, 30 to 45 minutes.
12. Preheat oven to 375 degrees F (190 degrees C).
13. Bake the bread in the preheated oven until the loaf sounds hollow when tapped and the crust is golden brown, about 30 minutes.
14. Spread top of hot loaf with butter to make a soft crust; let cool in the pan.

Sriracha Honey Chicken Legs

Ingredients:

2 pounds chicken legs, skin removed
2 tbsps. olive oil
1 1/2 tsps. ground thyme
1 1/2 tsps. garlic powder
1 tsp. ground paprika
1 tsp. salt
1 tsp. ground black pepper
3 tbsps. raw honey
3 tbsps. butter
2 tbsps. sriracha sauce 1
1/2 tbsps. soy sauce

Directions:

1. Preheat oven to 350 degrees F (175 degrees C).
2. Line a baking sheet with aluminum foil.
3. Combine chicken legs, olive oil, thyme, garlic powder, paprika, salt, and pepper in a large bowl. Mix chicken legs until coated and arrange on the baking sheet.
4. Bake in the preheated oven until an instant-read thermometer inserted near the bone reads 165 degrees F (74 degrees C), 45 to 50 minutes.
5. Combine honey, butter, sriracha sauce, and soy sauce in a saucepan over medium-low heat; cook and stir until butter is melted and sauce is smooth, about 5 minutes.
6. Pour sauce into a large bowl.
7. Transfer chicken from the baking sheet to the bowl using tongs; toss until coated with sauce.

Sriracha Honey Chicken Pizza

Ingredients:

4 tbsps. sriracha, divided
1 can (13.8 oz) refrigerated pizza crust
2 tbsps. olive oil
1/4 cup honey
2 tbsps. orange marmalade
1 tbsp. soy sauce
2 tsps. lime juice
1 cup cooked chicken, shredded
1-2 cups tomato sauce
1 1/2 cups manchego cheese, shredded
1 cup mozzarella cheese, shredded
4 slices cooked bacon, crumbled
4 green onions, chopped
Ranch dressing, for serving

Directions:

1. Preheat the grill to medium heat, and gather your ingredients.
2. Unroll the dough onto a heavily floured cookie sheet or pizza peel.
3. Spray the dough with cooking spray or rub olive oil over the dough.
4. Very carefully invert the dough from the pizza peel onto the grill.
5. Grill 2-3 minutes; flip and grill another 2 minutes.
6. Remove crust from the grill and place back on the pizza peel or a baking sheet.
7. In a small saucepan combine the honey, soy sauce, orange marmalade, lime juice, and 2 tbsps. Sriracha.
8. Bring to a boil and then reduce the heat. Simmer 5 minutes or until slightly thickened.
9. Once the sauce is thickened, remove from the heat and add the chicken.
10. Toss well.
11. Cover the pizza in tomato sauce, then drizzle with sriracha to taste.
12. Add the manchego cheese.
13. Add the chicken mixture and all of the sauce that may be left in the pot.
14. Add the crumbled bacon and mozzarella over the top.
15. Carefully slide the pizza back on the grill.
16. Close grill cover and cook over low-medium heat for 5-8 minutes, or until the cheese is melted. Remove from the grill, slice and eat immediately.

Sriracha Tuna Salad

Ingredients:

3 mini sweet peppers, or more to taste
1 (5 oz.) can tuna, or more to taste, drained and flaked
2 hard-boiled eggs, chopped
2 tbsps. Sriracha hot chili sauce
2 tbsps. mayonnaise
2 tbsps. honey mustard

Directions:

1. Mix tuna, eggs, and peppers in a bowl.
2. Stir sriracha, mayonnaise, and honey mustard into the tuna mixture.
3. Refrigerate tuna salad for 5 minutes.

Sriracha Ramen Noodle Soup

Ingredients:

2 tbsps. sriracha hot sauce
2 tbsps. sesame oil
1 small onion, diced
1 small roma tomato, diced
1 tbsp. ginger, grated
5 cloves garlic, minced
1/2 tsp. garlic powder
1/2 tsp. celery salt
4 cups vegetable broth
2 cups water
1 tbsp. soy sauce
1 tsp. rice vinegar
3 packages ramen noodles
1/2 cup scallions, chopped
1/2 cup cilantro, chopped
2 poached eggs (optional)

Directions:

1. Add the sesame oil and sriracha to a large stockpot and bring to a simmer over medium-heat.
2. Add the onion and tomato and cook for 4 minutes, stirring occasionally.
3. Add the ginger, garlic, and seasonings; cook for 2 minutes or until fragrant.
4. Add 2 cups of water and transfer mixture to a blender or food processor and pulse until smooth.
5. Return mixture to the pot and add the broth.
6. Bring to a simmer; add soy sauce and vinegar (if using), and simmer for 8-10 minutes. Taste and adjust seasoning as needed.
7. Add the ramen noodles to the broth and simmer for an additional 2-3 minutes, or until the noodles have softened.
8. Add the scallions, stir to combine. Remove pan from heat, ladle soup into bowls, and top with cilantro and eggs. Enjoy!

Sriracha Butter

Delicious on fresh corn on the cob, steak, veggies, baked potatoes and many other dishes.

Ingredients:

1 cup unsalted butter, at room temperature
2 tbsps. sriracha sauce, or to taste
1 tbsp. honey
5 cloves garlic, minced
1/4 tsp. salt
1 pinch ground black pepper

Directions:

1. Stir butter, sriracha sauce, honey, garlic, salt, and pepper with a rubber spatula in a bowl until smeared and blended together.
2. Scoop butter mixture onto a large piece of plastic wrap.
3. Roll up into a log; twist ends of the plastic together to tighten up the log.
4. Refrigerate until thoroughly chilled, about 1 hour.
5. Slice into 1/4-inch pats and place on a chilled plate.

Sriracha Scrambled Eggs

Ingredients:

1 tsp. sriracha sauce
2 eggs
1 tbsp. half-and-half
Salt and ground pepper to taste
2 tbsps. butter

Directions:

1. Beat eggs in a bowl with half-and-half, sriracha, salt, and pepper until smooth.
2. Melt butter in nonstick pan over medium-low heat, tilting the pan to cover surface entirely with butter.
3. Cook egg mixture in pan, stirring to slowly scramble eggs, until the eggs are fully set, 3 to 5 minutes.

Sriracha Whole Roasted Cauliflower

Ingredients:

1 tbsp. sriracha sauce
1/4 cup olive oil
1 lemon, zested and juiced
1 tbsp. ground cumin
1 tbsp. garlic powder
1 tbsp. Montreal steak seasoning
1 tsp. ground coriander
1 head cauliflower, leaves removed and base trimmed
1/4 cup freshly grated Parmesan cheese

Directions:

1. Preheat oven to 400 degrees F (200 degrees C).
2. Line a baking sheet with parchment paper.
3. Mix olive oil, lemon zest, lemon juice, Sriracha hot sauce, cumin, garlic powder, steak seasoning, and coriander together in a bowl.
4. Place cauliflower on the prepared baking sheet and brush olive oil mixture (or use your hands) over the entire cauliflower.
5. Roast in the preheated oven until cauliflower is lightly browned and dry, 30 to 40 minutes.
6. Cool cauliflower for 5 to 10 minutes.
7. Cut cauliflower into wedges and sprinkle Parmesan cheese over each.

Sriracha Cheese Cauliflower Bites

Ingredients:

1 head cauliflower, separated into florets
3 tbsps. olive oil
1 tsp. garlic powder
1 1/2 cups grated Cheddar cheese
Sriracha chili sauce, to taste
3 green onions, thinly sliced

Directions:

1. Preheat oven to 425 degrees F (220 degrees C).
2. Spray a 13x9-inch baking dish with non-stick cooking spray.
3. Place the cauliflower in a large mixing bowl.
4. Toss with the olive oil and garlic powder until thoroughly distributed.
5. Transfer the cauliflower mixture to prepared baking dish.
6. Bake in preheated oven 30 minutes.
7. Top with shredded cheese and bake until the cheese has melted, about 5 more minutes.
8. Top cheesy florets with sriracha sauce to taste and garnish with green onions. Serve with a cold glass of milk.

Sriracha Roasted Carrots

Ingredients:

1 pound carrots, quartered lengthwise and cut into 4-inch pieces
2 tbsps. coconut oil, melted
1/4 cup chicken broth
1 cup low-fat plain Greek yogurt
2 tsps. honey
2 tbsps. honey vanilla almond milk
1/2 tbsp. sriracha hot chili sauce

Directions:

1. Preheat oven to 375 degrees F (190 degrees C).
2. Lightly spray a rimmed baking sheet with cooking spray.
3. Toss carrots in a bowl with the oil to coat. Transfer to a prepared baking sheet in a single layer.
4. Roast in preheated oven for 15 minutes.
5. Pour chicken broth evenly over carrots; continue to cook until tender, about 10 minutes.
6. Mix yogurt, honey, almond milk, and sriracha sauce together in a bowl to make a thin drizzling sauce.
7. Transfer roasted carrots to a serving dish.
8. Drizzle with the honey-sriracha sauce.

Sriracha Steak Marinade

Ingredients:

1 tbsp. Sriracha hot chili sauce
1/2 cup olive oil
1/2 cup white vinegar
1/4 cup soy sauce
2 tbsps. Worcestershire sauce
1 tbsp. minced garlic
1 tbsp. dried onion flakes
1 tbsp. steak seasoning
1 steak of choice

Directions:

1. Combine olive oil, vinegar, soy sauce, Worcestershire sauce, garlic, onion flakes, Sriracha sauce, and steak seasoning in a re-sealable bag.
2. Add steak of your choice.
3. Marinade for at least an hour in the refrigerator.

Sriracha Avocado and Edamame Dip

Ingredients:

1 tbsp. Sriracha chile- sauce
6 oz. shelled edamame
1/2 onion, chopped
1/2 cup tightly packed cilantro
2 tbsps. olive oil
1 large avocado, peeled, pitted and cubed
1 lemon, juiced
Salt and pepper to taste

Directions:

1. Place the edamame, onion, cilantro, and olive oil into a food processor. Pulse until finely chopped.
2. Add the avocado, lemon juice, and chile-garlic sauce.
3. Season to taste with salt and pepper.
4. Puree until smooth. Refrigerate at least 30 minutes before serving.

Sriracha Chicken with Scallions

Ingredients:

1/2 cup Sriracha sauce, or more to taste
1 tbsp. vegetable oil, or as needed
3 chicken breasts, cut into cubes, or more to taste
1/4 cup rice vinegar
3 tbsps. soy sauce, or to taste
2 tsps. spicy mustard
1/2 tsp. chili oil
1/2 cup butter, or to taste
2 bunches green onions (scallions), chopped

Directions:

1. Coat the bottom of a skillet with vegetable oil and place over medium heat.
2. Saute chicken in the hot oil until no longer pink in the center, 5 to 10 minutes.
3. Add rice vinegar, soy sauce, mustard, chile oil, and Sriracha sauce, adding in exact order and waiting 1 minute between each addition for ingredient to layer.
4. Melt butter, stirring occasionally, into the chicken mixture creating a sauce, 2 to 3 minutes; lower heat to medium-low.
5. Add green onions and cook until slightly wilted, 2 to 3 minutes.

Sriracha Salt

Put in a pretty air tight jar and it makes a great gift.

Ingredients:

5 tsps. sriracha hot sauce
1/2 cup kosher salt

Directions:

1. Preheat oven to 350 degrees F (175 degrees C).
2. Line a baking sheet with parchment paper or a silicone mat.
3. Mix salt and sriracha hot sauce together in a small bowl.
4. Spread mixture onto the prepared baking sheet.
5. Place the baking sheet in the preheated oven and turn off the heat; let sit in the oven without opening the door, about 3 hours.
6. Stir salt mixture, breaking up any clumps. If not completely dry, repeat the process and check after 1 hour.
7. Place dry salt mixture in a food processor and pulse for a few seconds until clumps are gone.

Sriracha Pasta Bowl

Ingredients:

1/4 cup Sriracha chile sauce
1 (16 oz.) box spaghetti
1/4 cup honey
1 lime, juiced
2 tbsps. canola oil
2 cups thinly sliced mushrooms
2 med. carrots, cut into matchstick-size pieces
1 cup thinly sliced yellow or green bell pepper
1 cup sugar snap peas, halved lengthwise
1 (26 oz.) jar marinara Sauce
Sesame seeds
3 green onions, thinly sliced

Directions:

1. In a large pot bring 4 to 6 quarts of water to a rolling boil; add salt to taste and the Spaghetti; stir gently.
2. Cook pasta according to package directions; remove from heat and drain well.
3. Meanwhile, in a large skillet heat the oil over medium heat.
4. Add the mushrooms, carrots, bell pepper, and sugar snap peas.
5. Cook, stirring frequently, for 5 to 7 minutes or until tender; add the Spicy Marinara and stir; add the pasta and toss to combine.
6. Serve in bowls and top with a drizzle of the Sriracha-honey mixture, green onions, and a sprinkle of sesame seeds, if desired.

Scrambled Sriracha Peanut Butter Eggs

Ingredients:

1 tsp. sriracha sauce, or to taste
4 eggs
2 tbsps. peanut butter
2 tsps. minced fresh ginger
2 tsps. minced fresh garlic
1 tsp. seasoning sauce

Directions:

1. Whisk eggs, peanut butter, ginger, garlic, seasoning sauce, and sriracha sauce together in a small bowl.
2. Heat a nonstick skillet over medium heat.
3. Pour in egg mixture; cook and stir until scrambled and firm, about 5 minutes.

Korean Sriracha BBQ Sauce

Great on pok ribs.

Ingredients:

1 tbsp. Sriracha chile-garlic sauce
1 cup soy sauce
3/4 cup dark brown sugar
2 tbsps. minced garlic
1 tbsp. rice wine vinegar
1 tsp. grated fresh ginger
1 tsp. Asian (toasted) sesame oil
1 1/2 tsps. ground black pepper
1 tbsp. cornstarch 1 tbsp. water

Directions:

1. Stir soy sauce, brown sugar, garlic, rice wine vinegar, chile-garlic sauce, ginger, sesame oil, and black pepper together in a saucepan.
2. Bring to a boil.
3. Whisk cornstarch and water together in a small bowl until the cornstarch dissolves; pour into boiling soy sauce mixture.
4. Reduce heat to medium-low and cook until the sauce is thick, 3 to 5 minutes.

Sriracha Egg Salad

Ingredients:

2 tsps. Sriracha chile- sauce
8 oz. bacon
4 stalks celery, minced
1/2 cup mayonnaise
1/4 cup minced yellow onion
1 1/2 tbsps. sweet pickle relish
1 1/2 tbsps. prepared yellow mustard
1 1/2 tsps. dried dill weed
1 tsp. Worcestershire sauce
1 tsp. ground black pepper
1/2 tsp. paprika
1/4 tsp. salt
12 hard boiled eggs, shells removed

Directions:

1. Place the bacon in a large skillet and cook over medium-high heat, turning occasionally, until crispy, about 10 minutes.
2. Drain the bacon slices on paper towels and crumble once cooled.
3. Mix bacon, celery, mayonnaise, onion, relish, mustard, chile-garlic sauce, dill, Worcestershire, black pepper, paprika, and salt together in a large bowl; add eggs.
4. Break egg whites and yolks with a potato masher into the bacon mixture. Stir broken egg pieces into the salad.
5. Cover bowl with plastic wrap and refrigerate at least 1 hour.

Sriracha Black Bean Burgers

Ingredients:

1 tsp. Sriracha chile-garlic sauce
1 egg
1 1/2 tbsps. ground cumin
1 tbsp. chili powder
1 (16 oz.) can black beans, rinsed and drained
1 jalapeno pepper, minced
1 cup canned whole kernel corn, drained
3 cloves garlic, minced
1/2 cup bread crumbs 1/2 cup whole wheat flour
2 tbsps. vegetable oil

Directions:

1. Whisk egg, cumin, chili powder, and chile-garlic sauce together in a bowl.
2. Mash black beans in a separate bowl until they reach a paste-like consistency.
3. Stir jalapeno pepper, corn, and garlic through the black bean paste.
4. Mix the egg mixture into the black bean mixture.
5. Scatter the bread crumbs over the black bean mixture; mix with your hands to evenly incorporate.
6. Form the resulting mixture into 4 patties.
7. Pour flour into the bottom of a shallow dish; coat the patties in the flour to help them hold shape.
8. Heat vegetable oil in a skillet over medium heat. Cook the patties in hot oil until cooked through, about 5 minutes per side.

Sriracha Chickpea Curry

Ingredients:

Sriracha chile sauce
1 tbsp. coconut oil
1 med. yellow onion, thinly sliced
1 tbsp. minced fresh ginger root
4 cloves garlic, minced
2 tbsps. mild curry powder
1/4 tsp. red pepper flakes
2 1/2 cups vegetable broth
2 tbsps. reduced-sodium soy sauce or tamari
2 tbsps. pure maple syrup
2 tbsps. tomato paste
3/4 pound Yukon Gold potatoes, cut into
3/4-inch pieces
1 large carrot, sliced diagonally
1/4 inch thick
4 cups large cauliflower florets
1 (15 oz.) can chickpeas, rinsed and drained
1 cup coconut milk
1/4 cup chopped fresh cilantro, plus more for garnish
1/2 cup frozen peas
Salt to taste
Cooked basmati rice

Directions:

1. Melt coconut oil in a heavy 4-quart pot over medium heat.
2. Saute onion until lightly browned, 5 to 7 minutes.
3. Add ginger and garlic and saute until fragrant, about 30 seconds.
4. Add curry powder, pepper flakes, broth, soy sauce, maple syrup, and tomato paste and stir.
5. Add potatoes and carrot, cover pot, and bring to a boil.
6. Immediately reduce heat to a simmer and leave lid ajar.
7. Cook just until potatoes are tender, about 10 minutes.
8. Add cauliflower, chickpeas, coconut milk, and cilantro.
9. Stir gently to incorporate.
10. Return to simmer with lid ajar and simmer just until cauliflower is tender, 5 to 7 minutes.
11. Fold in peas and cook until heated through, about 1 minute.
12. Remove from heat and season with salt, if needed.

13. Serve with steamed basmati rice and, for those who'd like more heat, sriracha sauce.
14. Garnish with cilantro.

Sriracha Peanut Chicken

Ingredients:

1 1/2 tsps. curry powder
2 tbsps. Sriracha chili sauce
1 1/2 tsps. ground cayenne pepper, or to taste
1/2 tsp. ground cinnamon
2 tsps. soy sauce
1/2 pound uncooked spaghetti
1 tbsp. peanut oil
2 large skinless, boneless chicken breast halves, cut into 1-inch cubes
3 1/2 cups water
2 cups extra chunky peanut butter
4 green onions, coarsely chopped
1/2 cup chow mein noodles

Directions:

1. Combine curry powder, Thai chili garlic sauce, cayenne pepper, cinnamon, and soy sauce in a small bowl, and set aside.
2. Fill a saucepan with water, and bring it to a boil.
3. When the water is boiling, drop in the spaghetti and cook for 8 to 12 minutes, stirring occasionally, until tender.
4. Drain the spaghetti, and set aside.
5. Heat peanut oil in a skillet or wok over medium-high heat until barely smoking, and drop in the chicken.
6. Cook and stir 5 to 8 minutes, until the chicken is just beginning to brown and the inside is no longer pink.
7. Remove chicken from the skillet, and set aside.
8. Make the peanut sauce by stirring together peanut butter and 3 1/2 cups of water in a saucepan over medium heat until mixture is smooth and the peanut butter is melted.
9. Pour in the curry-chili sauce, and simmer, stirring occasionally, until the sauce is thickened, about 15 minutes.
10. To serve, place the noodles in a large bowl, top with chicken, and spoon the peanut sauce over the chicken.
11. Sprinkle the green onions over the dish, and garnish with chow mein noodles.

Sriracha Honey Popcorn

Ingredients:

2 tsp Sriracha hot chili sauce
1/2 cup honey
2 tbsp. butter
1/2 tsp salt
24 cups popped popcorn

Directions:

1. In a medium microwave-safe bowl, mix honey, Sriracha, butter and salt. Microwave on medium power for 30 to 40 seconds or until butter is melted and mixture is runny.
2. Place popcorn in a large bowl; drizzle honey mixture over popcorn.
3. Toss until evenly coated.

Sriracha Philly Cheesesteak Hot Dog

Ingredients:

Sriracha hot chili sauce
2 large white onions
1 lbs. shaved steak
4 oz. jack cheese grated or sliced
1/2 cup pickled jalapeno slices
4 hot dogs
4 hot dog buns

Directions:

1. Slice the onions and cook them on medium heat with a little oil and salt until very brown, about 25 minutes.
2. Meanwhile, in a very hot cast iron pan, sear the shaved steak.
3. Once cooked, add in the jalapenos and mix well. Add the cooked onions.
4. Remove from heat and add the cheese. Stir well.
5. Cook the hot dogs and put them into some oversized hot dog buns.
6. Top with your cheesesteak mixture.
7. Add a few jalapenos on top and a nice helping of sriracha hot chili sauce before serving!

Sriracha Garlic Cheese Pretzel Bites

Ingredients:

sriracha garlic cheese
1 cup PBR beer
1 lb extra-sharp cheddar cheese shredded
2 cloves garlic minced
1 tsp dry mustard powder
1/2 tsp freshly ground black pepper
1/2 tsp cayenne pepper
1/4 tsp salt
1/4 tsp sriracha hot chili sauce
1/4 tsp Worcestershire sauce

Pretzel Bites Ingredients:

4 tsp active dry yeast
1 tsp white sugar
1 1/4 cup warm water
5 cup flour
1/2 cup white sugar
1 1/2 tsp salt
1 tbsp vegetable oil
1/2 cup baking soda
4 cup hot water
1/4 cup kosher salt topping

Directions:

1. Pour beer into a bowl and whisk until beer loses its carbonation, about 30 seconds. Set aside.
2. Place shredded cheese into the work bowl of a food processor; add garlic, dry mustard powder, black pepper, 1/2 tsp. cayenne pepper, salt, hot sauce, Worcestershire sauce, and flat beer.
3. Process until smooth and creamy, pulsing a few times, scraping the sides, and blending for about 2 total minutes. Taste and adjust seasoning. If adding more seasoning, pulse a few times to mix.
4. Spoon small dollops of cheese onto parchment paper or Chocolate molds. Freeze solid.

5. Dissolve active dry yeast and 1 tsp. of white sugar into 1 1/4 cup warm water. Let sit for about 10 minutes, until creamy.
6. In a large bowl, mix together flour, sugar, and salt.
7. Make a well in the center and add oil and yeast mixture.
8. Mix together to form a dough, adding a small amount of water if dry. Knead for about 7-8 minutes.
9. Lightly oil large bowl and turn the dough inside the bowl to coat with the oil.
10. Cover and let rise until doubled, about an hour.
11. Preheat oven to 450 degrees F (230 degrees C).
12. Dissolve baking soda in hot water in a casserole dish (or large bowl).
13. When risen, place dough on a lightly floured surface and divide into 12 pieces. Roll each piece into a long rope the cut rope into 1 inch pieces.
14. Roll each 1 inch piece into a ball. Make indention with finger and insert cheese bit into indention.
15. Seal up the ball around the cheese.
16. Dip each stuffed pretzel into the baking soda solution and then place on a greased baking sheet. Sprinkle with kosher salt or cinnamon/sugar.
17. Bake in a preheated oven for about 7-8 minutes, or until browned.

Vegan Sriracha Chili

Ingredients:

3/4 cup sriracha hot chili sauce
1 yellow onion
4 garlic cloves
1 red pepper
1 1/2 tbsp chili powder
1 tbsp. cumin
28 oz. can black beans
28 oz. can white beans
28 oz. can kidney beans
28 oz. can diced tomatoes
1 cup frozen corn
1 cup water

Directions:

1. Peel and mince garlic.
2. Dice onion and pepper.
3. Place soup pot on medium heat.
4. Add olive oil and onions.
5. Sauté until translucent.
6. Add garlic and pepper.
7. Mix in chili powder, cumin and Sriracha and cook until vegetables are soft.
8. Add remaining ingredients and let simmer for 20 minutes.

Sriracha and Cream Cheese Wontons

Ingredients:

1 tbsp. sriracha hot chili sauce
1/2 (4 oz.) block cream cheese softened
1 tsp chives finely sliced
16 wonton wrappers
 sweet and sour or sriracha sauce for dipping
hot oil for frying

Directions:

1. In a large bowl, mix the cream cheese, chives and sriracha sauce.
2. Arrange the wonton wrappers on a flat surface.
3. Dollop about a tsp. of the cream cheese mixture in the center of each wrapper.
4. Dip your finger in a little water and run along the edges of the wrappers.
5. Pull the edges together and twist to seal. Continue until all the wontons are filled and sealed.
6. Bring the oil to high heat. In batches, fry the wonton bombs until golden brown and crispy, about two minutes per batch (or less).
7. Continue until all the wonton bombs are fried. Place them on paper towels to drain.

Sriracha Macaroni and Cheese

Sauce Ingredients:

3 cups whole milk
1/2 cup unsalted butter
1/2 cup all-purpose flour
2 tsps. kosher salt

Pasta Ingredients:

2-3 tbsps. Sriracha sauce, plus more for drizzling
3/4 pound dried elbow pasta
1 tbsp. minced fresh ginger
2 1/2 tbsps. unsalted butter, at room temperature
2 cups grated Havarti
1 cup chopped green onions (both green and white parts)
3/4 cup Japanese bread crumbs

Directions:

1. Heat the milk in a pot over medium heat until it just starts to bubble, but is not boiling, 3-4 minutes.
2. Remove from the heat.
3. Heat the butter over medium heat in a separate, heavy bottomed pot. When the butter has just melted, add the flour and whisk constantly until the mixture turns light brown, about 3 minutes.
4. Remove from heat.
5. Slowly pour the warm milk, about 1 cup at a time, into the butter-flour mixture, whisking constantly.
6. It will get thick when you first add the milk, and thinner as you slowly pour in the entire 3 cups.
7. This is normal.
8. Once all the milk has been added, set the pot back over medium-high heat, and continue to whisk constantly.
9. In the next 2-3 minutes the sauce should come together and become silk and thick.
10. Use the spoon test to make sure it's ready.
11. Dip a metal spoon into the sauce-if the sauce coats the spoon and doesn't slide off like milk, you know it's ready.
12. Add the salt and stir to combine.
13. Preheat oven to 400 degrees F.
14. Cook the pasta in salted boiling water until a little less than al dente.

15. Drain, rinse with cold water, and drain the pasta again.
16. Mash together the ginger and butter in a small bowl until fully combined.
17. Add the mac sauce, cheese, and ginger butter to a large heavy-bottomed pot and cook over medium heat.
18. Stir until the cheese is barely melted, about 3 minutes.
19. Add the sriracha and the cooked pasta and continue cooking while stirring continuously until the dish is nice and hot, another 5 minutes.
20. Add the green onions and stir to fully combine.
21. Pour the mac into a 14-inch casserole pan and sprinkle with panko.
22. Bake until hot and bubbly and the topping is golden, about 20 minutes. Remove from the oven and drizzle with more sriracha. Spoon into bowls and serve.

Sriracha Corn Chowder

Ingredients:

1/2 cup Sriracha, plus more for garnish
8 ears fresh sweet corn, husked
2 tbsps. olive oil
2 red bell peppers, seeded and diced
2 red onions, diced
5 cloves garlic, minced
6 cups vegetable stock
3 sprigs fresh thyme
2 bay leaves
1 cup heavy cream
Salt and freshly ground black pepper
Smoked paprika, for garnish
Torn leaves of fresh cilantro or flat-leaf parsley, for garnish

Directions:

1. Roast 4 ears of corn over a direct flame (on a preheated grill or over a gas burner) until the corn kernels begin to blacken, turning every few minutes until all sides have roasted. After the roasted ears have cooled, scrape the kernels from the cobs, and reserve.
2. Heat the oil in a large Dutch oven over medium heat. Add the bell peppers and onions and cook until softened slightly, 5 to 7 minutes.
3. Meanwhile, scrape the corn kernels from the remaining 4 ears of corn. Add the raw corn kernels and garlic, and cook until the garlic is aromatic, 1 to 2 minutes.
4. Add the stock, Sriracha, thyme, and bay leaves. Bring to a boil, then lower the heat and simmer for 45 minutes.
5. About 10 minutes before the soup is finished, gently heat the cream over low heat, keeping it just below a simmer.
6. Once the soup has cooked for 45 minutes, discard the thyme and bay leaves. Puree the soup using a food processor or blender.
7. Mix in the warm cream and add the reserved roasted corn.
8. Cook for an additional 3 to 5 minutes, until thoroughly heated.
9. Season with salt and pepper to taste.
10. Ladle the soup into bowls and garnish with a few lines of Sriracha, a generous sprinkle of smoked paprika, and torn cilantro or parsley leaves.

Sriracha Brussels Sprouts

Ingredients:

1 lb. Brussels sprouts
1 1/2 tbsp. Sriracha
1 tbsp. apple cider vinegar
1 tbsp. lemon juice
1 tbsp. brown sugar
2 cloves garlic
1 medium shallot
1 tbsp. butter
1/2 tbsp. olive oil
1 tsp salt
1/2 tsp pepper
1 1/2 oz. creamy goat cheese

Directions:

1. Start by washing the Brussels sprouts and then cutting the base off and quartering them.
2. Mix the Sriracha, apple cider vinegar, lemon juice, and brown sugar together. Pour this mixture over the Brussels sprouts and mix everything up to make sure all the sprouts are coated. Let everything soak together for 10 to 15 minutes.
3. When you're cutting the shallots up, cut them across the grain to form little shallot rings, then cut these in half.
4. Mince the garlic.
5. Using a pan large enough to cook the Brussels sprouts sauté the garlic and shallots in the olive oil and butter on high heat.
6. You'll want to get some caramelization going here.
7. Once you get some caramelization going on the shallots add the Brussels sprouts to the pan and cook on high heat for a couple of minutes.
8. Turn the heat down to medium high and stir the pan every few minutes to keep everything from burning.
9. Once the sprouts have finished cooking, which usually takes 8 to 12 minutes, add the salt and pepper and serve with a nice creamy goat cheese.

Sriracha Chocolate Ice Cream

Ingredients:

3 Tbsp. Cocoa Powder
1/2 tsp. Ground Cinnamon
2 tsp. Sriracha
2 1/2 Tbsp. Maple Syrup
1 Can Full-Fat Coconut Milk

Directions:

1. Place the cocoa powder, cinnamon, sriracha, and maple syrup into a small bowl and whisk together until clumpy.
2. Slowly incorporate the coconut milk into the mixture, about 2 tbsp. of it at a time, so that it stays smooth.
3. After the coconut milk is fully whisked in, put the bowl into a freezer for 25 minutes.
4. Once the mixture is cool, pour it into your ice cream maker and wait for it to full freeze up.

Sriracha Tomato Soup

Ingredients:

2 tbs. sriracha chili sauce
2 (28 oz.) cans tomato soup
2 cup chicken stock
3 cloves of garlic, minced
4 tbsps. butter
1/3 cup heavy cream
Salt and pepper to taste

Directions:

1. Blend the tomatoes and chicken stock.
2. Melt the butter in a large saucepan and sauté the garlic.
3. Pour in the tomato blend and then the rest of the ingredients.
4. Let the soup simmer for about 15 minutes and serve.

Honey-Sriracha Ham Glaze

Ingredients:

1/2 cup honey
2 tbsp. brown sugar packed
1 - 2 tbsp. sriracha hot chili sauce
1 clove garlic finely chopped

Directions:

1. In small bowl, stir together all ingredients.
2. Brush over ham the last 45 minutes of baking.
3. Bake ham according to package directions.
4. Serve and enjoy!

Carrot Coconut Soup

Ingredients:

sriracha hot chili sauce
4 tbsp. unsalted butter
1 lb. carrots peeled & chopped
kosher salt
freshly ground black pepper
2 cups low-sodium chicken broth
1 14 oz. can unsweetened coconut milk
1 tbsp. sambal oelek

fresh cilantro for serving

Directions:

1. Melt butter in a large saucepan over medium-high heat.
2. Add carrots and onion, season with salt & pepper, and cook, stirring often, until carrots are softened, 15-20 minutes.
3. Stir in broth, coconut milk, and sambal oelek.
4. Bring to a boil, reduce heat, and simmer, stirring occasionally, until vegetables are very soft and liquid is slightly reduced, 40-45 minutes.
5. Let soup cool slightly, then puree in a blender or with an immersion blender until smooth.
6. Reheat in the saucepan, thinning with water to desired consistency; season with salt & pepper.
7. Divide soup among bowls, drizzle with sriracha and top with cilantro.

Sriracha Burger

Ingredients:

3 pounds ground beef
1/4 cup soy sauce
10 tbsps. Sriracha
4 tsps. freshly ground black pepper
14 slices thick-cut bacon
2 large sweet onions
3/4 cup blue cheese dressing
8 sesame seed buns
8 thick slices Swiss cheese
1 large beefsteak tomato, sliced
Arugula or romaine lettuce

Directions:

1. In a large mixing bowl, combine ground beef, soy sauce, 5 tbsps. Sriracha, and pepper.
2. Do not over mix. Form the mixture into 8 patties, and set aside, on a parchment-lined baking sheet, covered, in the refrigerator.
3. Preheat a charcoal or gas grill to medium-high heat.
4. In a medium frying pan over medium-low heat, cook the bacon, turning as necessary.
5. While the bacon is cooking, peel and quarter the onions. Cut each section into 1/4-inch slices.
6. Once the bacon is cooked through and slightly crispy, remove the slices from the pan, cut each in half crosswise, and drain onto paper towels, reserving the remaining bacon fat in the pan.
7. Cook the sliced onions in the bacon fat over medium-low heat until they caramelize, 20 to 25 minutes.
8. Grill the burgers, turning once, 4 to 4 1/2 minutes on each side or until a meat thermometer registers 130° to 135 degrees F for medium-rare. While the burgers are cooking, in a small bowl, combine the blue cheese dressing with the remaining 5 tbsps. Sriracha.
9. Lightly toast the buns on the grill during the last minute of cooking time.
10. spread the blue cheese mixture on both halves of each hamburger bun.
11. Stack a burger patty, Swiss cheese slice, bacon, caramelized onions, tomato slice, and a small handful of arugula between each hamburger bun.

Sriracha Peanut Butter Fudge

Ingredients:

1/3 cup Sriracha sauce
3/4 cup crunchy peanut butter
1/3 cup honey
1/3 cup white sugar

Directions:

1. In a small sauce pan, bring the Sriracha sauce, honey and sugar to a temperature of 240 degrees F – 245 degrees F over medium heat.
2. Remove from heat and thoroughly stir in the peanut butter.
3. Pour into an aluminum foil lined shallow dish and let cool.
4. Cut up and serve.

Sriracha Chicken Breasts

Ingredients:

2 tbsps. sriracha chili sauce with garlic
4 chicken breast halves, skin on and bone in
1/2 cup soy sauce
1/4 cup teriyaki sauce
1 stalk lemongrass -- chopped
1/4 onion -- finely minced
2 cloves garlic -- finely minced
2 tbsps. black bean sauce
1 tbsp. ginger -- finely grated
1 tsp. hot pepper flakes
2 tbsps. rice wine -- (aji-mirin)
2 tbsps. sweet soy sauce
(use molasses if unavailable)
1 tbsp. rice wine vinegar
2 tbsps. sesame seeds
3 tbsps. sesame oil
1 tbsp. Korean stir fry sauce
1 tbsp. hoisin sauce
1 tbsp. chili oil
1 tbsp. cilantro, finely chopped

Directions:

1. Place all ingredients except the chicken in a large Ziploc baggie, and mix to blend all ingredients together.
2. Add Chicken pieces and distribute evenly in the bag.
3. Seal, place on plate and refrigerate at least 2 hours, turning every 30 minutes.
4. Heat the grill for low coals.
5. Grill the chicken, turning frequently and basting with marinade, for approximately 30 minutes or until done.
6. The sugars in the marinade will char quickly, so covering the grill will reduce the flames and charring.

Sriracha Chex Mix

Ingredients:

¼ cup Sriracha
6 cups mixed Chex cereal
1 1/2 cups cheddar-flavored crackers Cheez-Its or Cheese Nips)
1 /2 cups pretzels
1 cup peanuts
4 tbsp. unsalted butter
2 tbsp. soy sauce
1 tsp. grated ginger
1 tsp. grated garlic (or garlic powder)

Directions:

1. Preheat your oven to 250 degrees F.
2. Mix the Chex, crackers, pretzels, and peanuts in a large bowl.
3. In a small microwave-safe bowl, combine the butter, Sriracha, soy sauce, ginger, and garlic.
4. Microwave the mixture in 15-second intervals until the butter is melted. Stir to combine.
5. Spread the mixture evenly over a large rimmed baking sheet.
6. Bake for an hour, stirring every 15 minutes, until the Chex Mix is crunchy.
7. Allow to cool. Once cool, store in an airtight container.

Sriracha Bacon-Wrapped Onion Rings

Ingredients:

1 large brown onion
20 slices of raw bacon

Dipping Sauce Ingredients:

1/4 cup honey, heated in microwave for about 15 seconds
4 tbsp. sriracha
1 tbsp. soy sauce

Glaze Ingredients:

3-4 tbsp. sriracha
1/4 cup honey
1 tbsp. soy sauce
1 tsp. cornstarch + 1 tbsp. water
Chopped cilantro for garnish

Directions:

1. Remove outer skin of onion and slice rings about 1/2 inch thick.
2. Separate rings, keeping two together for each separated ring (doubling up preserves the onion ring shape).
3. To making dipping sauce, combine honey, sriracha and soy sauce in a small bowl.
4. Brush each onion lightly with the sauce. 3.
5. For each ring, you will need about 2 pieces of bacon.
6. Wrap bacon around onion rings, tucking ends of bacon into the last wrapped section and then placing a toothpick through at the places where each bacon ends, in order to secure during cooking.
7. Dunk each bacon wrapped ring in sauce and then place on a large baking sheet lined with parchment paper. 5.
8. Preheat oven to 400 degrees F.
9. Bake onions for about 30 minutes.
10. Remove from oven and flip onions over, cooking for another 20 minutes or until bacon is crispy.
11. Check in on the onions about 5 minutes before they are done to make sure your bacon is not charring too much.

12. You may need to lower temperature or move to a lower shelf in oven for the last few minutes if your bacon is charring too fast before it's finished being crispy.
13. If your bacon is crispy but is not charred at all, you may need to adjust the temperature higher (about 15-25 degrees) for the last 2-3 minutes until you get a slight char. 6.
14. Remove bacon onion rings from oven and let bacon cool slightly and crisp up further.
15. Add sriracha, honey and soy sauce to a small saucepan and bring to a low boil.
16. In a small bowl, completely dissolve cornstarch in water and then add to boiling mixture.
17. Stir until sauce is thickened and then turn off stove.
18. Brush a light layer of glaze on each of the finished bacon rings before serving.
19. Garnish with chopped cilantro if desired.

Pork Belly With Sriracha Glaze

Ingredients:

2 lb. pork belly

Marinade Ingredients:

1/4 cup soy sauce
1/3 cup rice wine
2 tbsp. brown sugar
2 cloves garlic, minced

Spice Rub Ingredients:

2-3 tbsp. five spice powder

Sriracha Glaze Ingredients:

1/4 cup honey
1 tbsp. soy sauce
3 tbsp. sriracha sauce
1 tsp cornstarch + 1 tbsp. water.

Directions:

1. The night before, score the pork belly skin, careful not to cut into the meat, but you do want to cut deeply into the skin.
2. The skin is scored by slicing lines diagonally across, about 1 inch apart, and then slicing lines diagonally the opposite way (see photo above).
3. Rub spice powder onto skin (about 1-2 tbsp.), making sure to rub on the surface and the crevices.
4. In a bowl, mix marinade ingredients.
5. Using a pan that just fits the pork belly, pour in the marinade and then put in the pork belly.
6. You only want the marinade to cover the meat and not touch the skin.
7. Place in fridge, uncovered, overnight, so that the skin is able to dry out.
8. On the day of cooking, preheat oven to 375F.
9. Completely line a roasting pan with foil for easier clean-up.
10. Pour water in about 1/2 in deep.
11. Rub an additional 1 tbsp. of spice powder onto pork belly skin.
12. Place a rack in the roasting pan and put pork belly on top, making sure it doesn't touch the water.

13. Gently use additional foil to tent the top of the pork belly. Bake for approximately 30-40 minutes until meat is finished cooking.
14. Remove pork belly from oven and remove foil tent.
15. If your pork belly is uneven in height, prop something under the lower parts so that it is an even height to help the pork belly skin crisp evenly.
16. Turn heat up to 425 degrees F and place pork belly back into oven.
17. Bake for another 15-20 minutes until all the skin blisters.
18. Watch carefully to make sure skin does not burn and overcook.
19. The skin needs to blister to stay crunchy.
20. If desired, make and brush skin with glaze before serving.
21. The pork belly is flavorful on its own as well.
22. The glaze adds some extra flavor to the skin, but it also overpowers the subtle meat flavor so the meat might taste a little bland, and you may want to reserve some glaze for dipping if you use the glaze.
23. To make glaze, add honey, soy sauce and sriracha to a small saucepan and bring to a low boil.
24. Completely dissolve cornstarch in water in a small bowl and then add to saucepan.
25. Keep the glaze at a low boil and stir until sauce thickens.

Buffalo Sriracha Hummus

Ingredients:

2 tbsps. Sriracha hot sauce
1 (15 oz.) can chickpeas, drained
1/2 tsp. cumin
3/4 tsp. smoked paprika
1/4 tsp. cayenne pepper
3/4 tsp. sea salt
3 cloves garlic
2 tbsps. tahini
1 tbsp. lemon juice
1/2 cup roasted peppers
2 tbsps. olive oil

Directions:

1. Blend everything except olive oil together in a food processor or high speed blender.
2. Once well combined, add olive oil and mix again.
3. Pour into a bowl for dipping.
4. Serve with a drizzle of olive oil and cayenne or some fresh cilantro.

Sriracha Honey Almonds

Ingredients:

4 cups (1 lb.) raw whole almonds
1/4 cup sriracha sauce
1/4 cup honey or maple syrup
3 tbsp. olive oil
1/2 + 1/2 tsp. salt

Directions:

1. Preheat the oven to 350 degrees F.
2. Mix the nuts, sriracha sauce, honey or maple syrup, oil and half tsp. salt properly in a bowl.
3. Spread them in an even layer on a foil lined baking sheet.
4. Bake them for 10 min.
5. Take it out, stir the almonds around and bake for another 10 min.
6. Cool the almonds completely.
7. Sprinkle half tsp. of sea salt on the almonds.
8. If they are not crunchy put them back in to the oven for another 5 min.

Sriracha-Buttered Shrimp

Ingredients:

2 tbsps. butter
6 tbsps. Sriracha
3 cloves minced garlic
1 pound head-on shrimp
1 tbsp. lemon zest
2 tbsps. minced fresh mint
2 tbsps. minced fresh basil

Directions:

1. Whip butter with Sriracha and melt in skillet.
2. Sauté minced garlic in it and toss in shrimp. Just before they're done, add lemon zest and mint and basil and let them wilt.

Sriracha Marinara and Meatballs

Meatballs Ingredients:

1 lb. ground pork
1 lb. ground white-meat turkey
2 pkgs. (10 oz. each) frozen spinach, thawed and squeezed dry
1/3 cup plain dried breadcrumbs
2 large egg whites
3/4 tsp. dried oregano
Coarse salt and ground pepper
Nonstick cooking spray

Sauce Ingredients:

2 tsps. extra-virgin olive oil
1 small yellow onion, diced small
2 garlic cloves, roughly chopped
2 cans (28 oz. each) crushed tomatoes
1/4 cup Sriracha sauce
1 lb. spaghetti or other long pasta
1/2 cup parsley leaves, chopped, for serving

Directions:

1. Heat broiler, with rack in top position.
2. Place pork, turkey, spinach, breadcrumbs, egg whites, oregano, 1 1/2 tsps. salt, and 1/2 tsp. pepper in a large bowl.
3. With your hands, mix to combine; roll into 40 1-inch meatballs.
4. Arrange meatballs on a rimmed baking sheet.
5. Lightly coat with cooking spray. Broil until golden brown, 10 minutes, rotating sheet halfway through.
6. In a large heavy pot, heat oil over medium.
7. Add onion and garlic and cook, stirring occasionally, until onion is translucent, 6 minutes.
8. Add tomatoes and Sriracha and bring to a simmer.
9. Add meatballs and simmer 10 minutes.
10. In a large pot of boiling salted water, cook pasta according to package instructions.
11. Drain pasta, add to pot with sauce and meatballs, and toss to coat.
12. Sprinkle with parsley and serve.

Shrimp Sriracha Cocktail Sauce

Ingredients:

1 lb shrimp shelled and deveined + cooked and chilled
1/2 cup ketchup
2 tbsp sriracha
1/2 tsp soy sauce
1/2 tsp Worcestershire sauce
1 tsp prepared horseradish
1 tsp lemon juice
1 pinch black pepper to taste
parsley fresh, for garnish

Directions:

1. In a medium bowl, whisk together ketchup, sriracha, soy sauce, Worcestershire sauce, horseradish, lemon juice, and pepper to taste.
2. Pour sriracha cocktail sauce in a small bowl.
3. Serve with cooked shrimp.

Sriracha Ketchup

Ingredients:

1/2 cup ketchup
2 tbsps. sriracha
1 tbsp. honey
2 tsps. freshly squeezed juice from 1 lime
2 tsps. chopped cilantro leaves
1 tsp. rice vinegar

Directions:

1. Whisk together ketchup, sriracha, honey, lime juice, cilantro, and vinegar in a small bowl.

Sriracha Mayo

Great with French fries.

Ingredients:

3 tbsps. mayo.
1 tbsp. Sriracha chili sauce
1 tsp. lemon/lime juice.
1/4 tsp. soy sauce

Directions:

1. In bowl, combine ingredients until smooth.
2. Use as dip or spread for your favorite dishes.

Sriracha Deviled Eggs

Ingredients:

12 eggs
6 tbsps. mayonnaise
2 tsps. Dijon mustard
4 tsps. Sriracha hot sauce
2 tsps. squeezed lime juice
2 tsps. chopped fresh cilantro
Kosher salt
Freshly ground black pepper
Pickled carrots or daikon, for garnish (optional)
Finely chopped fresh cilantro leaves, for garnish (optional)

Directions:

1. Hard-boil the eggs; cool, peel, and halve them; and carefully remove the yolks. Reserve the whites.
2. 2Combine the egg yolks, mayonnaise, Dijon, Sriracha, lime juice, and cilantro in a medium nonreactive bowl.
3. Season well with salt and pepper, then mix well until the yolks are broken up and the ingredients are evenly incorporated.
4. 3Evenly pipe or spoon the yolk mixture into the reserved egg white halves.
5. Top with pickled carrots or daikon and chopped cilantro leaves.

Sriracha Salad Dressing

Pour over your favorite greens.

Ingredients:

1 tsp. Sriracha chili sauce, plus extra to taste.
3 tbsps. fresh lime juice
4-5 tbsps. white vinegar.
1/4 cup extra virgin olive oil.
3 tbsps. honey.
1 tbsp. sugar.
1 large clove garlic, pressed + minced.
1/4 tsp. salt.

Directions:

1. Roll your lime [or lemon!] on the countertop to help release the juices, then slice and squeeze into a small bowl.
2. Measure out 3 tbsps. and set aside.
3. Combine citrus juice with vinegar, oil, honey, sugar, garlic, Sriracha, and salt and whisk to incorporate.

Sriracha Nachos

Sriracha Beef Ingredients:

1/3 cup sriracha
Oil for cooking
1 small onion, diced
2 small shallots, diced
2 cloves of garlic, minced
1 lb lean ground beef
2 tbsps. soy sauce

Nachos Ingredients:

1 (14 oz.) bag tortilla chips
1 cup sliced green onions
3 jalapeños, sliced
1 red pepper, diced
1 1/2 cups grated cheddar
1 1/2 cups grated mozzarella
1 cup roughly chopped cilantro
Sour cream, salsa and guacamole, if desired

Directions:

1. Preheat the oven to 400 degrees F.
2. Line a baking sheet with foil or parchment paper.
3. In a skillet over medium-high, heat up a bit of oil.
4. Add the onion and shallots and cook until translucent.
5. Add the garlic and cook for another 2 minutes.
6. Add the beef and brown.
7. Drain off the fat and stir in the sriracha and soy sauce.
8. Place a single layer of chips on your foil-lined baking sheet.
9. Sprinkle on some sriracha beef, green onions, jalapeños, red pepper, cheddar and mozzarella.
10. Repeat until all of your ingredients are gone.
11. Bake for 5-7 minutes, or until the cheese is gooey and melted.
12. Top with the cilantro and enjoy with sour cream, salsa and guacamole if desired.

Sriracha Tuna Tartare

Ingredients:

2 tsps. Sriracha sauce
2 sesame rice crackers or shrimp chips
 Canola oil for frying (if using sesame crackers)
12 oz. tuna sushi-grade, finely diced
1/2 English cucumber finely diced
1/2 shallot finely diced
1 tbsp. sesame oil
1 tbsp. soy sauce
1 tsp. olive oil extra-virgin
 Kosher salt
2 tbsps. cilantro leaves chopped

Directions:

1. If using sesame crackers, add about an inch of oil to a large, shallow saute pan and set over high heat until it registers 350 F on a candy thermometer. Use tongs to place one sesame cracker sheet in the oil and fry for about 30 seconds; the cracker will puff up.
2. Remove from the oil, place on a plate lined with a paper towel, and let cool. Repeat with the second sheet.
3. Once the sheets are cool, break them into large pieces. Set aside.
4. Combine the tuna, cucumber, and shallot in a medium bowl and set aside. In a small bowl, combine the sesame oil, soy sauce, Sriracha sauce, and olive oil and stir to combine.
5. Season to taste with salt.
6. Pour the marinade over the tuna and mix gently.
7. Garnish with the cilantro and serve with the fried sesame rice crackers or shrimp chips.

Sriracha Chicken Salad

Ingredients:

1 tsp. Sriracha sauce
1 boneless, skinless chicken breast
2 tbsp. mayonnaise
1/4 cup onion, finely minced*
Chili flakes to taste

Directions:

1. In a pot of boiling water, boil the chicken breast until it is no longer pink in the middle.
2. Shred the chicken into thin threads.
3. In a bowl, mix the shredded chicken, mayonnaise, Sriracha, and chili flakes together.

About the Author

Laura Sommers is **The Recipe Lady!**

She is the #1 Best Selling Author of over 80 recipe books.

She is a loving wife and mother who lives on a small farm in Baltimore County, Maryland and has a passion for all things domestic especially when it comes to saving money. She has a profitable eBay business and is a couponing addict. Follow her tips and tricks to learn how to make delicious meals on a budget, save money or to learn the latest life hack!

Visit her Amazon Author Page to see her latest books:

amazon.com/author/laurasommers

Visit the Recipe Lady's blog for even more great recipes and to learn which books are **FREE** for download each week:

http://the-recipe-lady.blogspot.com/

Subscribe to The Recipe Lady blog through Amazon and have recipes and updates sent directly to your Kindle:

The Recipe Lady Blog through Amazon

Laura Sommers is also an Extreme Couponer and Penny Hauler! If you would like to find out how to get things for **FREE** with coupons or how to get things for only a **PENNY**, then visit her couponing blog **Penny Items and Freebies**

http://penny-items-and-freebies.blogspot.com/

Other books by Laura Sommers

- **Recipe Hacks for Saltine Crackers**
- **Recipe Hacks for Canned Biscuits**
- **Recipe Hacks for Canned Soup**
- **Recipe Hacks for Beer**
- **Recipe Hacks for Peanut Butter**
- **Recipe Hacks for Potato Chips**
- **Recipe Hacks for Oreo Cookies**
- **Recipe Hacks for Cheese Puffs**
- **Recipe Hacks for Pasta Sauce**
- **Recipe Hacks for Canned Tuna Fish**
- **Recipe Hacks for Dry Onion Soup Mix**
- **Recipe Hacks for Dry Ranch Salad Dressing and Dip Mix**
- **Recipe Hacks for a Box of Mac & Cheese**
- **Recipe Hacks for Instant Mashed Potato Flakes**
- **Recipe Hacks for Pancake Mix**
- **How to Shop for Penny Items**

May all of your meals be a banquet
with good friends and good food.

Made in the USA
San Bernardino, CA
28 March 2019